The Law of Process

John C. Maxwell

Student's Guide

Published by Nelson Word Multi Media Group
A division of Thomas Nelson Publishers

Copyright © 1999 by Thomas Nelson Publishers

Printed in the United States of America
ISBN 0-7852-9672-7

For Information
Call Thomas Nelson Publishers 1-800-251-4000

About the Author

John C. Maxwell, called America's expert on leadership, is the founder of The INJOY Group, an organization dedicated to helping people maximize their personal and leadership potential. He is also founder of the nonprofit organization EQUIP. Each year Maxwell speaks in person to more than 250,000 people and influences the lives of more than one million people through seminars, books, and tapes. He is the author of twenty-two books, including, *Becoming a Person of Influence, The Success Journey, Developing the Leader Within You, Developing the Leaders Around You, The 21 Irrefutable Laws of Leadership*, and *Failing Forward.*

Introduction

As I travel and speak to organizations and individuals, people frequently ask me to define the essentials of leadership. "If you were to take everything you've learned about leadership over the years and boil it down into a short list," they ask, "what would it be?"

My book, *The 21 Irrefutable Laws of Leadership*, is my answer to that often-asked question. It has taken me a lifetime to learn these principles and I desire to communicate them to you as simply and clearly as possible. And it sure won't hurt if we have some fun along the way.

One of the most important truths I've learned over the years is this: Leadership is leadership, no matter where you go or what you do. Times change. Technology marches forward. Cultures vary from place to place. But the true principles of leadership are constant—whether you're looking at the citizens of ancient Greece, the Hebrews in the Old Testament, the armies of the last two hundred years, the rulers of modern Europe, the pastors in local churches, or the businesspeople of today's global economy. Leadership principles stand the test of time. They are irrefutable.

As we explore together **The Law of Process**, I'd like you to keep in mind four ideas:

- **The laws of leadership can be learned.** Some are easier to understand and apply than others, but every one of them can be acquired.

- **The laws can stand alone.** Each law complements all the others, but you don't need one in order to learn another.

- **The laws carry consequences.** Apply the laws, and people will follow you. Violate or ignore them, and you will not be able to lead others.

- **These laws are the foundation of leadership.** Once you learn the principles, you have to practice them and apply them to your life.

My desire is to see you succeed, and live life to your maximum potential by increasing your leadership ability. You can read my book and watch this video series in a few days, but it will take you a lifetime to maximize the laws in your own life.

Every session in this video course consists of three parts:

1. **"Case in Point" and opening discussion**
2. **Video Notes**
3. **Application and Assessment**

"Case in Point" contains a brief story that demonstrates the Law of Process in real life. Next, as you watch the video presentation, you will want to make a note of your impressions and personal reflections. Finally, the Application and Assessment section will take you more deeply into making this principle a part of your daily life, as well as assessing your current practices.

As you watch this video and work through these materials as a group, I encourage you to share your lives and learn from one another. All of us have experienced both success and failure as we grow in our ability to lead others.

Whether you are a follower who is just beginning to discover the impact of leadership or a natural leader who already has followers, you can become a better leader. The Law of Process—as well as all the other laws—is a tool ready to pick up and use to help you achieve your dreams and add value to other people.

Table of Contents

Leadership develops daily, not in a day.

The secret to Anne Scheiber's success was that she spent most of her life building her worth. Whether her stock's values went up or down, she never sold it off with the thought, *I'm finished building; now it's time to cash out.* She was in for the long haul, the *really* long haul.

Perseverance pays.

Theodore Roosevelt helped create a world power, won a Nobel Peace Prize, and became the President of the United States. But today you wouldn't even know his name if he hadn't known the Law of Process.

To lead tomorrow, learn today.

I focus my time and energy on doing what makes a positive impact in the lives of people. But I've also made a lot of mistakes along the way—more than most people I know. Every success and every failure has been an invaluable lesson in what it means to lead.

The Law of Process
Session One

Leadership Develops Daily, Not in a Day

The Law of Process
Session One

Case in Point

Imagine the surprise of Norman Lamm, the president of Yeshiva University in New York City, when he found out that Anne Scheiber, a little old lady whom he had never heard of—and who had never attended Yeshiva—left nearly her entire estate to the university.

"When I saw the will, it was mind blowing, such an unexpected windfall," said Lamm. "This woman has become a legend overnight."

The estate Anne Scheiber left to Yeshiva University was worth $22 million![1] How in the world did a spinster who had been retired for fifty years build an eight-figure fortune?

Anne Scheiber was 101 years old when she died in January of 1995. For years she had lived in a tiny, run-down, rent-controlled studio apartment in Manhattan. The paint on the walls was peeling, and the old bookcases that lined the walls were covered in dust. Rent was $400 a month.

Scheiber lived on Social Security and a small monthly pension, which she started receiving in 1943 when she retired as an auditor for the Internal Revenue Service. She hadn't done very well at the IRS. More specifically, the agency hadn't done right by her. Despite having a law degree and doing excellent work, she was never promoted. And when she retired at age fifty-one, she was making only $3,150 a year.

"She was treated very, very shabbily," said Benjamin Clark, who knew her as well as anyone did. "She really had to fend for herself in every way. It was really quite a struggle."

Scheiber was the model of thrift. She didn't spend money on herself. She didn't buy new furniture as the old pieces she owned became worn out. She didn't even subscribe to a newspaper. About once a week, she used to go to the public library to read the *Wall Street Journal.*

By the time she retired from the IRS in 1943, Anne Scheiber had managed to save $5,000. She invested that money in stocks. By 1950, she had made enough profit to buy 1,000 shares of Schering-Plough Corporation stock, then valued at $10,000. And she held on to that stock, letting its value build. Today, those original shares have split enough times to produce 128,000 shares, worth $7.5 million.[2]

The secret to Scheiber's success was that she spent most of her life building her worth. Whether her stock's values went up or down, she never sold it off with the thought, *I'm finished building; now it's time to cash out.* She was in for the long haul, the *really* long haul. When she earned dividends—which kept getting larger and larger—she reinvested them. She spent her whole lifetime building. While other older people worry that they may run out of funds before the end of their lives, the longer she lived, the wealthier she became. When it came to finances, Scheiber understood and applied the Law of Process.

Opening discussion/reflection:
1. What qualities of Ms. Scheiber do you admire?
2. Does her story make you feel uncomfortable? If so, why?
3. How do you think this story demonstrates the leadership process?

Video Notes

Some people are born with leadership _____.

_____
_____
_____
_____
_____

Some people are _____ how to lead.

_____
_____
_____
_____
_____
_____

The only appreciable asset any organization has is _____.

_____
_____
_____
_____

Video Notes

Session One
Application and Assessment

Leadership Is Like _____— It Compounds!

What matters most is what you do day by day over the long haul. Although it's true that some people are born with greater natural gifts than others, the ability to lead is really a collection of skills, nearly all of which can be learned and improved.

Do you agree with the above statement? Why or why not?

_____

_____

_____

What investments are you making today that will enhance your leadership ability in the future?

_____

_____

_____

_____

Are you a better leader today than you were one year ago? Why or why not?

_____

_____

_____

_____

Becoming a leader is a lot like investing successfully in the stock market. If your hope is to make a fortune in a day, you're not going to be successful.

Leaders Are Learners. To Lead Tomorrow, _____ Today

In a study of ninety top leaders from a variety of fields, leadership experts Warren Bennis and Burt Nanus made a discovery about the relationship between growth and leadership: ***"It is the capacity to develop and improve their skills that distinguishes leaders from their followers."*** Successful leaders are learners. And the learning process is ongoing, a result of <u>self-discipline</u> and <u>perseverance</u>. The goal each day must be to get a little better, to build on the previous day's progress.

What have you learned in the last six months that has made you a better leader?

_____

_____

_____

_____

_____

How have you applied what you have learned in the last six months?

_____

_____

_____

_____

_____

_____

"Like the horizons for breadth and the ocean for depth, the understanding of a good leader is broad and deep."

Proverbs 25:3
(*The Message*)

> *"To be conscious that you are ignorant of the facts is a great step to knowledge."*
>
> **Benjamin Disraeli**

The Four Phases of Leadership

PHASE 1
I DON'T KNOW WHAT I DON'T KNOW

Most people fail to recognize the value of leadership, believing that leadership is only for the few at the top of the corporate ladder. This point was driven home for me when a college president shared with me that only a handful of students signed up for a leadership course offered by the school. Why? Only a few thought of themselves as leaders. If the others had realized that leadership is influence, and that in the course of each day most individuals usually try to influence at least four other people, they might have wanted to learn more about the subject. It's unfortunate, because as long as a person doesn't know what he doesn't know, he doesn't grow.

PHASE 2
I KNOW WHAT I DON'T KNOW

Usually at some point in life, we are placed in a leadership position only to look around and discover that no one is following us. That's when we realize that we need to *learn* how to lead.

That's what happened to me when I took my first leadership position in 1969. I had captained sports teams all my life and had been the student government president in college, so I thought I was already a leader. But when I tried to lead people in the *real* world, I found out the awful truth.

That prompted me to start gathering resources to learn. I also had another idea: I wrote to the top ten leaders in my field and offered them one hundred dollars for a half hour of their time so that I could ask them questions. (That was quite a sum for me in 1969.) For the next several years, my wife, Margaret, and I planned every vacation around where those people lived. And my idea really paid off. Those men shared insights with me that I could have learned no other way.

PHASE 3
I GROW AND KNOW IT STARTS TO SHOW

When you recognize your lack of skill and begin the daily discipline of personal growth in leadership, exciting things start to happen.

In five years, you'll see progress as your influence becomes greater. In ten years, you'll develop a competence that makes your leadership highly effective. And in twenty years, if you've continued to learn and grow, others will likely start asking you to teach them about leadership. And they'll look at each other and say, "How did he/she suddenly become so wise?"

PHASE 4
I SIMPLY GO BECAUSE OF WHAT I KNOW

When you are in phase 3, you can be pretty effective as a leader, but you have to think about every move you make.

"The secret of success in life is for a man to be ready for his time when it comes."

Benjamin Disraeli

As long as a person doesn't know what he doesn't know, he doesn't grow.

However, when you get to phase 4, your ability to lead becomes almost automatic. And that's when the payoff is larger than life. But the only way to get there is to obey the Law of Process and pay the price.

The Four Phases of Leadership Growth

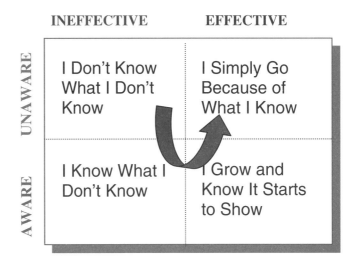

Write your name in the box that you think currently best describes your growth phase in leadership.

Closing discussion:

In your small group, share your leadership growth goals:
a. For the next year
b. In five years
c. In ten years

(Be sure to write these goals in your notes for future reference.)

Application and Assessment Notes

_____

_____

_____

_____

_____

_____

_____

_____

_____

_____

_____

_____

_____

_____

_____

_____

_____

_____

_____

_____

_____

_____

_____

_____

_____

_____

_____

_____

Application and Assessment Notes

_____

_____

_____

_____

_____

_____

_____

_____

_____

_____

_____

_____

_____

_____

_____

_____

_____

_____

_____

ENDNOTES

[1] Sharon E. Epperson, "Death and the Maven," *Time*, 18 December 1995.
[2] James K. Glassman, "An Old Lady's Lesson: Patience Usually Pays," *Washington post*, 17 December 1995, H01.

The Law of Process
Session Two

Perseverance Pays

The Law of Process
Session Two

Case in Point

President Theodore Roosevelt was an outspoken man of action and advocate of the vigorous life. While in the White House, he was known for his regular boxing and judo sessions. He also took vigorous horseback rides and long strenuous hikes.

"TR" was a tough leader, both physically and mentally, but he did not start that way. America's cowboy president was born in Manhattan to a prominent and wealthy family. As a child, he was smallish and of ill health. He had debilitating asthma, very poor eyesight, and was strikingly thin. When he was twelve, Roosevelt's father told him, "You have the mind, but you have not the body, and without the help of the body the mind cannot go as far as it should. You must *make* the body."

Roosevelt began investing time *every day* to build his body as well as his mind, and he did that for the rest of his life. He worked out with weights, hiked, ice-skated, hunted, rowed, boxed and rode horseback.

Roosevelt did not become a great leader overnight, either. His journey to the presidency was one of slow continual growth. As he served in various government positions, he kept learning and improving himself. In time, he became a strong leader with extraordinary accomplishments.

During TR's presidency, the U.S. emerged as a world power with a first-class navy. He oversaw the building of the Panama Canal. He negotiated peace between Russia and Japan, winning a Nobel Peace Prize in the process. When people questioned his leadership—since he had become president when McKinley was assassinated—he campaigned and was reelected by the largest majority of any president before him.

When Roosevelt completed his term as president in 1909, he immediately traveled to Africa where he led a scientific expedition sponsored by the Smithsonian institution. He also co-led a group to explore the uncharted River of Doubt in Brazil. It was a great learning adventure he said he could not pass up. "It was my last chance to be a boy," he later said. He was 55 years old at the time.

On January 6, 1919, at his home in New York, Theodore Roosevelt died in his sleep. At the time, then Vice-President Marshall said, "Death had to take him sleeping, for if Roosevelt had been awake, there would have been a fight." When they removed him from his bed, they found a book under his pillow. Up to the very end, TR was still striving to learn and improve himself—still practicing the Law of Process.

Opening discussion/reflection:
1. What impresses you most about this former president? _____

_____

2. Are you intentional (proactive) or are you more random (reactive) in your approach to life?

_____

Video Notes

One of the problems in leadership development is that we overestimate the _____, underestimate the _____.

THE EVENT
Encourages _____

_____ people

Is a _____ issue

_____ people

Is _____

THE PROCESS
Encourages _____

_____ people

Is a _____ issue

_____ people

Is _____

LEADERSHIP IS MANY FACETED:

(1) _____

_____

(2) _____

_____

(3 _____

_____

(4) _____

_____

(5) _____

_____

(6) _____

_____

(7) _____

_____

(8) _____

_____

The secret of our success is found in our _____ _____.

Video Notes

Session Two

Application and Assessment

Developing the Law of Process

SET YOUR MIND AND HEART ON _____
_____.

Whether you call it a goal, vision or plan makes little difference. The key is moving forward, one step at a time, one day at a time, intentionally, over a long period of time.

It is not important to try to see the end of your life's journey at this point—none of us really knows the final score before the game is over. It *is* important, however, that you know the current score and continue adding points to your account in life.

Michael Jordan never focused on how many points he would have at the end of a game, but he was fiercely focused on continually scoring more points throughout the game. This is the Law of Process. Jordan also knew that to score more points during the game, he must practice for hours before the game! This is also the Law of Process. Together this combination wins games, builds companies, grows churches, and creates success in life.

When Dan came as an intern, I thought, "I'm never going to do this again. Now when I look at Dan, I think, "Whoa! It's a miracle! Leadership can be taught."

DEVELOP EFFECTIVE PERSONAL

_____.

(Health, religion, family, etc.)

As we discovered in the life of Theodore Roosevelt, personal habits can have an important impact on our growth.

Our long-term goals and priorities are always reflected in our daily routine.

What personal habits in your life are helping you to become a better leader?

_____

_____

_____

_____

What personal habits are hindering you from becoming a better leader?

_____

_____

_____

_____

What personal habit do you need to begin to become a better leader?

_____

_____

_____

_____

You don't become a leader at a leadership conference. You become a person with leadership resources.

> *We confuse success with the recognition of success.*
>
> *Success is not a destination. It is a daily thing.*
>
> *So is failure.*

LOOK AT THE _____ _____.

The big picture of the Law of Process teaches us not to focus only on the game at hand, but the whole season—not only the bottom line for this quarter, but the whole fiscal year. Whether you are an athlete, business person, or minister, the Law of Process requires you to look at the big picture of progress.

Evaluate your current status.

Are you moving forward?

_____

_____

_____

_____

What brought you this far?

_____

_____

_____

_____

Are you satisfied with your current situation?

_____

_____

_____

_____

What is working?

_____

_____

_____

_____

What is not working?

_____

_____

_____

What must you do to improve?

_____

_____

_____

_____

SHARE WITH OTHERS OF _____ _____.

The Law of Process, though lonely at times, is never realized alone. It is lonely because while others are "playing," you continue to invest your time into personal growth. It is not realized alone because no one is so self-sufficient that they can monitor their own progress completely. It is like walking in the forest; without a guide or a compass, you will walk in circles.

Champions are always a result of the process.

Champions don't become champions in the ring—they are merely recognized there!

The Law of Process is all about the daily steps necessary to become a better leader and continue moving forward. Set your sights forward, and take action every day.

Create your own personal "insiders" group.

Pull together a small group of people—perhaps three to five—who become your "insiders." Trust these people and give them permission to speak candidly with you about any part of your life, and, in particular, the progress that you are making.

This group may consist of anyone who knows and cares about you! They could be:
- colleagues, family, friends, or a combination of all three;
- people who live in your city or across the country;
- experts in your field or those who know nothing about your field.

You may meet in person, by phone, or by letter. You may meet monthly or twice a year.

You can see how flexible this is, but you *must* have an "insiders" group to help guide you through the process. You may not always agree with their input and always follow their advice, but if you have the right group, you will always sharpen your thinking and improve your personal growth.

Who might you consider for your group?

_____

_____

_____

AVOID THE _____ _____ LIKE THE PLAGUE!

The comfort zone kills process. We all grow at different rates and speeds, and our growth is greater in some seasons of our life than others.

I do *not* want to paint a picture of a paranoid workaholic caught in the performance trap. Celebrating victories and smelling the roses is important to health and enjoying life. But if you stay there very long, the lethal weapon of comfort will destroy the process of growth.

Being in the comfort zone does not mean you are not working hard. You may be working very hard. You can be in the comfort zone and be working into the wee hours of every morning.

The comfort zone is doing the *same* things, with the *same* people, in the *same* ways, over and over. Watch for this and stay out of this danger zone.

LEARN FROM YOUR _____.

Mistakes are one of the greatest learning tools available. Mistakes are great, as long as you do not make the same one twice. If you are not making mistakes, you are not stretching yourself enough. Without mistakes, you cut short the process of growth as a leader.

> *If you are still smelling the roses long after the petals have withered, you are in danger of the comfort zone.*
>
> *If you do not cultivate the rose garden, there will be no more roses to smell.*

You do not plan to make a mistake, but you will improve your plans because of your mistakes. I call this failing forward!

Closing discussion:

1. What mistakes have you made in the last 90 days?

_____

_____

_____

_____

2. What did you learn?

_____

_____

_____

_____

3. What will you do differently in the future as a result of learning from your mistakes?

_____

_____

_____

_____

Application and Assessment Notes

Application and Assessment Notes

_____

_____

_____

_____

_____

_____

_____

_____

_____

_____

_____

_____

_____

_____

_____

_____

_____

_____

_____

_____

_____

_____

_____

_____

_____

_____

_____

_____

_____

_____

_____

_____

_____

The Law of Process
Session Three

To Lead Tomorrow, Learn Today

Session Three

Case in Point

I have the privilege of teaching leadership across the country and around the globe, and I often get the opportunity to talk with people who are attending one of my conferences for a second, third, or even fourth time. At a recent conference here in the United States, a man in his late fifties whom I had met several years before came up and spoke to me during a break. He grabbed my hand and shook it vigorously. "Learning leadership has changed my life," he said. "But I sure wish I had heard you twenty years ago."

"No, you don't," I answered with a chuckle.

"What do you mean?" he said. "I would have achieved so much more! If I had known these leadership principles twenty years ago, I'd be in a totally different place in life. Your leadership laws have fueled my vision. They've given me the desire to learn more about leadership and accomplish my goals. If I'd learned this twenty years ago, I could have done some things that I had never even dreamed possible."

"Maybe you would have," I answered. "But twenty years ago, I wouldn't have been able to teach them to you. It has taken me my entire lifetime to learn and apply the laws of leadership to my life."

As I write this, I am fifty-one years old. I've spent more than thirty years in professional leadership positions. I've founded four companies. And I focus my time and energy on doing what makes a positive impact in the lives of people. But I've also made a lot of mistakes along the way—more than most people I know. Every success and every failure has been an invaluable lesson in what it means to lead.

Opening discussion/reflection:

In our previous session, we learned that leadership has many facets. It includes skills, experience, maturity, relationships, timing, culture, training, and attitude.

Take a few moments to consider leaders you have known or read about. Share with your group what specific traits you believe make this person an effective leader.

_____

_____

Video Notes

Our daily agenda reveals our:

(1) _____ (4) _____ (7) _____

(2) _____ (5) _____ (8) _____

(3) _____ (6) _____ (9) _____

Video Notes

Session Three
Application and Assessment

> *"The heights of great men reached and kept,*
> *Were not attained by sudden flight,*
> *But they, while their companions slept,*
> *Were toiling upwards in the night."*
> Winston Churchill

Pursue relationships with people who _____ you and encourage you.

All my life I have pursued relationships with people who stretch me as a leader and as a person. I am grateful for all the wonderful input I have received over the years, so much so, that now I invest a large portion of my life into stretching others.

I have learned some things along the way that may be helpful to you as you pursue others to help you learn and grow.

Regarding mentors:

- Pursue people who are further down the road of life's experiences than you are.

(Name?) _____

- Pursue others who have experienced success in your area of interest.

(Name?) _____

- Pursue others who are interested in helping you.

(Name?) _____

- Pursue others only if their character matches their competency.

(Name?) _____

Regarding the learner (you):

- Be willing to learn on their terms and on their schedule.

  Yes? _____ No? _____

- Be willing to spend money to learn and grow.

  Yes? _____ No? _____

- Prepare yourself, and respect their time by writing down questions to ask them.

- If you will be in their presence, but not able to ask questions, jot down a few key thoughts anyway.

- Always express your gratitude for the ways in which they help you.

- Pass on what you learned, gained, and experienced to someone else.

- As soon as you are able, contribute into their life. Do not worry about big and small. Gratitude is a state of the heart, not an amount monitored on some scoreboard.

- Make a commitment to do this all your life. It is the process that counts!

Be willing to spend money and time to learn and grow!

Pigs and humans! Nothing in common?

Surgeons are using pig valves in human heart operations!

Whether politics and music or science and business, mix it up and see what you can learn.

Practice connecting and _____ what you learn and experience.

Independent learning experiences are not nearly as valuable as connected and integrated learning experiences. In other words, we learn much about one idea, project, or field from what appears to be a completely unrelated area. For example, I just read an interesting little book that compared church growth to the art of growing healthy bonsai trees! What in the world do the two have in common? After reading the book, I saw they had much in common!

Another interesting example is the connection of attending a ball game or a concert in which the fans exuberantly express their every thought, feeling, and emotion in a number of wild ways—and a church worship service where it seems like every possible measure is taken to hold everything inside as the people worship God. A wise pastor will integrate the two experiences to learn what he can to bring life into his/her worship service. (I am not suggesting hot dogs and Cracker Jacks! . . . but then again . . .)

Have you recently had a similar experience with seemingly unrelated issues? Share it with your group.

_____

_____

_____

school

TRAVEL
Rain
Rain
Snow
FAMILY
Picnics
Cats
Art
Music
Picnics
CHURCH
Dogs

Life Application

Think of learning as a funnel. The narrow end represents the point of application in your life experience. The large end, however, is open to a great deal more than you can handle at one time, and as it pours down through the focal point of your personal application, you "mix it up" and benefit from the combined variety of input.

No matter where you are in life, or what you face, giving up is not the answer. Whether you are 22 or 72, you have hope and potential!

A 98-year-old woman in Massachusetts named Jean just graduated from high school, after a 90-year break!

When she was eight, she left school to help her parents raise the other kids. Now she is considering college. Jean understands process!

Never _____!

My friend Zig Ziglar tells the story of how he was broke and in debt at age 45. Today he is one of the most successful Christian businessmen I know. He chose not to give up.

No matter where you are in life, or what you face, giving up is not the answer. Whether you are 22 or 72, you have hope and potential!

Have you ever given up on something important to you (or been tempted to)? What was the result of your decision to either leave or stay?

_____

_____

_____

_____

_____

_____

Closing discussion:

Use this time to ask and discuss any final questions you may have regarding the Law of Process.

Application and Assessment Notes

_____

_____

_____

_____

_____

_____

_____

_____

_____

_____

_____

_____

_____

_____

_____

_____

_____

_____

_____

_____

_____

_____

_____

_____

_____

_____

_____

_____

_____

_____

_____

Application and Assessment Notes

Additional resources to help you apply
The Law of Process

Learning the 21 Laws of Leadership Video curriculum
John C. Maxwell
This videocassette program is the most challenging leadership-training program available on the market today. Filled with wisdom, wit and wonderful examples, the 21 laws allow you to bring your entire leadership team together to develop a shared vision, a corporate purpose and a united effort. If teamwork is a high value for you, this teaching video program is a must.
Contents: 6 interactive videos and an easy-to-use leader's guide to make teaching more effective.
Price: $99.95   Product Code: B2143K

The Success Journey Book
John C. Maxwell
John Maxwell reveals three keys to success and spells out practical principles anyone can use. You will discover how to prepare for the journey, create your own road map, overcome detours, include your family in your dreams and build professional relationships that will benefit others as well as yourself.
Price: $19.99   Product Code: B2133

**To order these resources or for more information, please
call 1-800-333-6506 or visit us on the web at *www.injoy.com*.**

OTHER EZ LESSON PLANS

The EZ Lesson Plan was designed with the facilitator in mind. This new format gives you the flexibility as a teacher to use the video as the visual and then refer to the facilitator's guide for the questions….and even better, the answers. It is designed for a four-week study, communicated by our top authors and it is totally self contained. **Each EZ Lesson Plan requires the student's guides to be purchased separately as we have maintained a very low purchase price on the video resource.**

Please visit your local Christian bookstore to see the other titles we have available in the EZ Lesson Plan format. We have listed some of the titles and authors for your convenience:

EZ LESSON PLANS NOW AVAILABLE:

The 10 Commandments of Dating   **Ben Young and Dr. Samuel Adams**

Are you tired of pouring time, energy, and money into relationships that start off great and end with heartache? If so, you need The 10 Commandments of Dating to give you the hard-hitting, black-and-white, practical guidelines that will address your questions and frustrations about dating. This guide will help you keep your head in the search for the desire of your heart.
EZ Lesson Plan ISBN: 0-7852-9619-0   **Student's Guide ISBN: 0-7852-9621-2**

Extreme Evil: Kids Killing Kids   **Bob Larson**

Kids are killing kids in public schools! Kids are killing their parents! What is causing all of this evil in our younger generation? Do we need prayer back in the schools…or do we need God to start in the home? Bob Larson gets us to the root of these evils and brings us some of the answers we are looking for in this new video assisted program.
EZ Lesson Plan ISBN: 0-7852-9701-4   **Student's Guide ISBN: 0-7852-9702-2**

Life Is Tough, but God Is Faithful   **Sheila Walsh**

Sheila takes a look at eight crucial turning points that can help you rediscover God's love and forgiveness. Showing how the choices you make affect your life, she offers insights from the book of Job, from her own life, and from the lives of people whose simple but determined faith helped them become shining lights in a dark world.
EZ Lesson Plan ISBN: 0-7852-9618-2   **Student's Guide ISBN: 0-7852-9620-4**

Why I Believe   **D. James Kennedy**

In this video, Dr. D. James Kennedy offers intelligent, informed responses to frequently heard objections to the Christian faith. By dealing with topics such as the Bible, Creation, the Resurrection and the return of Christ, Why I Believe provides a solid foundation for Christians to clarify their own thinking while becoming more articulate in the defense of their faith.
EZ Lesson Plan ISBN: 0-7852-8770-9   **Student's Guide ISBN: 0-7852-8769-5**

The Lord's Prayer   **Jack Hayford**

Why do we say "Thy Kingdom come?" What does "Hallowed be Thy Name" mean? Do we really practice "Forgive us our debts as we forgive our debtors?" Pastor Jack Hayford walks you through verse by verse and then applies his great scripture to our personal lives. This study will put "meaning to the words" you have just been saying for years.

EZ Lesson Plan ISBN: 0-7852-9442-2   **Student's Guide ISBN: 0-7852-9609-3**

How To Pray   **Ronnie Floyd**

Whether you are a rookie in prayer or a seasoned prayer warrior, this video kit will meet you where you are and take you to another level in your prayer life. You may have been raised in a Christian home where prayer was a normal, daily exercise. You may have attended church all of your life, where the prayers of the people and the minister were as common as the hymns that still ring in your ears. Yet such experiences do not guarantee that you know how to pray. With simple, yet profound prose, Dr. Floyd declares, "prayer occurs when you depend on God, prayerlessness occurs when you depend on yourself."

EZ Lesson Plan ISBN: 0-8499-8790-3   **Student's Guide ISBN: 0-8499-8793-8**

EZ LESSON PLANS COMING SOON:

Healing Prayer   **Reginald Cherry, M.D.**

"Prayer is the divine key that unlocks God's pathway to healing in both the natural and supernatural realms of life." In Healing Prayer, he explores the connection between faith and healing, the Bible and medicine. Cherry blends the latest research, true stories, and biblical principles to show that spirit-directed prayers can bring healing for disease.

EZ Lesson Plan ISBN: 0-7852-9666-2   **Student's Guide ISBN: 0-7852-9667-0**

Jesus and The Terminator   **Jack Hayford**

From the **E-Quake** Series comes the EZ Lesson Plan that is the focal point of the Book of Revelation. Pastor Hayford sets the stage for the fight against the Evil One when the end of time comes upon us. There is no greater force than that of Jesus and now viewers will see Him become triumphant again in this battle that is evident.

EZ Lesson Plan ISBN: 0-7852-9601-8   **Student's Guide ISBN: 0-7852-9658-1**

The Law of Process   **John C. Maxwell**

Leadership develops daily, not in a day. This law, taken from **The Twenty One Irrefutable Laws of Leadership** is the first of the series to be placed into an individual study. Take each opportunity as it comes along and find the answer in a way only strong leaders would do it….by processing it. John explains how and why "Champions don't become champions in the ring…they are merely recognized there."

EZ Lesson Plan ISBN: 0-7852-9671-9   **Student's Guide ISBN: 0-7852-9672-7**

Forgiveness   **John MacArthur**

In this three-session EZ Lesson Plan, noted biblical scholar John MacArthur provides an insightful look at forgiveness. MacArthur not only reminds us that we are called to grant forgiveness to those who sin against us, but he also teaches the importance of learning to accept the forgiveness of others.

EZ Lesson Plan ISBN: 0-8499-8808-X   **Student's Guide ISBN: 0-8499-8809-8**

Andy Griffith - Honesty   **Systems Media, Inc.**

For generations, stories have been used to teach universal truths. In keeping with this time-honored tradition, the new three-volume Andy Griffith Bible Study Series has been developed, which uses the classic stories of Mayberry to illustrate biblical truths. In *Honesty*, the first volume of the series, learn from Andy, Opie, and the gang as they struggle with, and learn from, everyday life situations.

EZ Lesson Plan ISBN: 0-8499-8815-2   **Student's Guide ISBN: 0-8499-8816-0**

Becoming A Woman of Grace   **Cynthia Heald**

This is a newly formatted product built around a message that only Cynthia Heald could deliver to us. Women have proven to be the stronger of the sexes in prayer, empathy and faith. Cynthia leads this women's group study on how a woman can become A Woman of Grace through prayer, obedience to God and other practices of their lives. This EZ Lesson Plan will bring the components of this publishing product to one, self-contained format ready to start small groups.

EZ Lesson Plan ISBN: 0-7852-9706-5   **Student's Guide ISBN: 0-7852-9707-3**

Created To Be God's Friend   **Henry Blackaby**

Henry Blackaby being born a man of God, living his life as a man of God, teaches us how all of us are created equal in being God's friend. No Christian need live without a keen sense of purpose, and no believer need give up on finding daily closeness with God.

EZ Lesson Plan ISBN: 0-7852-9718-9   **Student's Guide ISBN: 0-7852-9719-7**

Resurrection   **Hank Hanegraaff**

In this definitive work, popular Christian apologist Hank Hanegraaff offers a detailed defense of the Resurrection, the singularly most important event in history and the foundation upon which Christianity is built. Using the acronym F.E.A.T., the author examines the four distinctive, factual evidences of Christ's resurrection--Fatal torment, Empty tomb, Appearances, and Transformation--making the case for each in a memorable way that believers can readily use in their own defense of the faith.

EZ Lesson Plan ISBN: 0-8499-8798-9   **Student's Guide ISBN: 0-8499-8799-7**

The Murder of Jesus   **John MacArthur**

To many, the story of Christ's crucifixion has become so familiar that is has lost its ability to shock, outrage or stir any great emotion. In *The Murder of Jesus*, John MacArthur presents this pivotal moment in the life of Jesus in a way that forces the viewers to witness this event in all its power. The passion of Christ is examined chronoligically through the lens of the New Testament with special attention given to Jesus' words on the cross, the miracles that attended the crucifixion, and the significance of Christ's atoning work.

EZ Lesson Plan ISBN: 0-8499-8796-2   **Student's Guide ISBN: 0-8499-8797-0**

Fresh Brewed Life   **Nicole Johnson**

God is calling us to wake up, to shout an enthusiastic "Yes" to life, just as we say "Yes" to our first cup of coffee each morning. Nothing would please Him more than for us to live fresh-brewed lives steeped with His love, filling the world with the marvelous aroma of Christ. The EZ Lesson Plan will provide humor, vignettes, and in depth study to small groups all over on this topic.

EZ Lesson Plan ISBN: 0-7852-9723-5   **Student's Guide ISBN: 0-7852-9724-3**

The Law of Respect   **John C. Maxwell**

We are taught from our parents to respect others. Our business practices are to be ones of respecting others ideas, thoughts and mainly their motivations. We tend to get caught up in the daily routines, but if we do not respect those around us and the ones we work with, our success will be held at a low ebb. John Maxwell is a leader's leader.

EZ Lesson Plan ISBN: 0-7852-9756-1   **Student's Guide ISBN: 0-7852-9757-X**

The Ten Commandments   **Jack Hayford**

We are all taught the Ten Commandments early in our Christian walk. Dr. Jack Hayford now takes us one step farther and teaches us each of these commandments by a video-assisted method. Dr. Hayford teaches us to honor our fathers and our mothers by first teaching us to honor our Lord. All ten commandments will be taught over a four-session study. Studies with the comprehensive study material sold separately.

EZ Lesson Plan ISBN: 0-7852-9771-5   **Student's Guide ISBN: 0-7852-9772-3**

Fit To Be a Lady   **Kim Camp**

Kim Camp shows moms how to make it through the difficult years of parenting pre-adolescent daughters by nurturing their girls in the love and grace of God--the source of all self-worth and confidence. Camp examines such topics as peer influences, music and the media, sex and purity, and diet and exercise.

EZ Lesson Plan ISBN: 0-8499-8827-6   **Student's Guide ISBN: 0-8499-8828-4**